Drum Pad Stick Skin

You're the soloist with these trio, quartet and quintet groups as they play rock, soul, ballad, jazz, latin and pop renditions of these great songs.

Listen to the recorded drummer. Then add your solo to complete the recording on the version minus drums.

Includes the complete drum charts for all the songs.

The Beat Goes On
Song for My Father
Watermelon Man
John Brown's Body
Terry's Tune
The Girl from Ipanema
Comin Home Baby

MMO

5006

The Kenny Smith Trio
The Mike Abene Quartet
The Mauricio Smith Quintet
Dee Dee Bridgewater, vocals

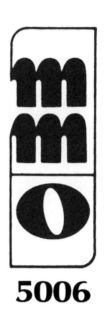

5006

MMO CD 5006
MMO Cass. 4075

DRUMPADSTICKSKIN

Band No. Complete Version		Band No. Minus Bass	Page No.
1	The Beat Goes On	8	4
2	Song For My Father	9	6
3	Watermelon Man	10	8
4	John Brown's body	11	10
5	Terry's Tune	12	12
6	Comin' Home Baby	13	14
7	The Girl From Ipanema	14	15

The Beat Goes On

Words and Music by SONNY BONO

Song For My Father

Music by HORACE SILVER
Words by JON HENDRICKS

Watermelon Man

Words and Music by HERBIE HANCOCK

Piano Intro

MMO CD 5006
Cassette 4075

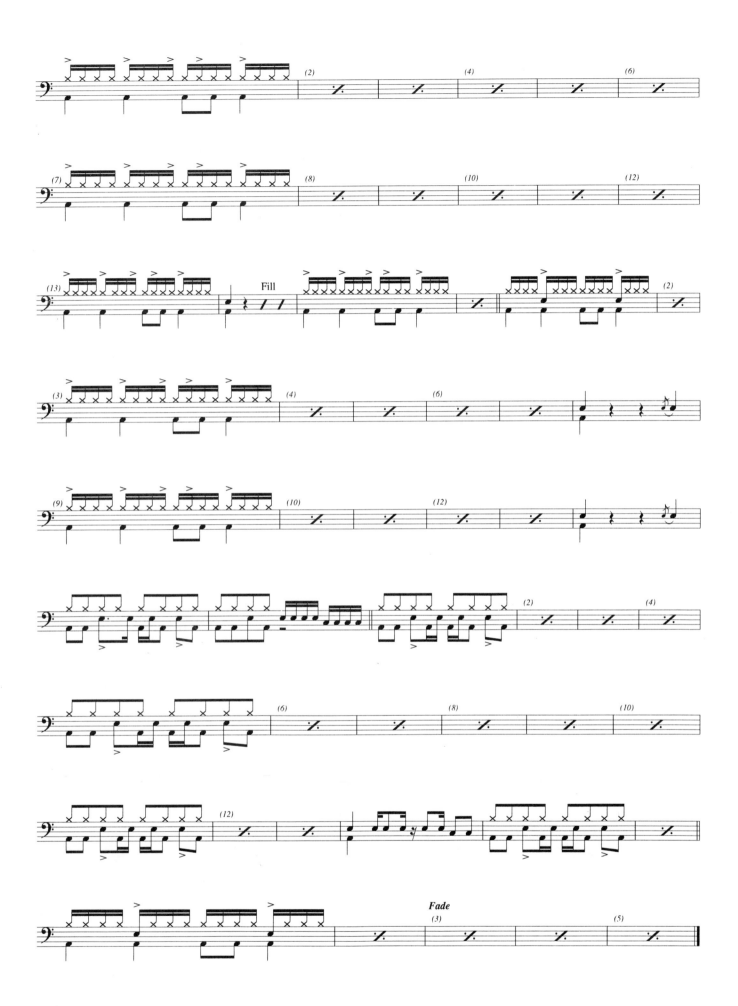

John Brown's Body

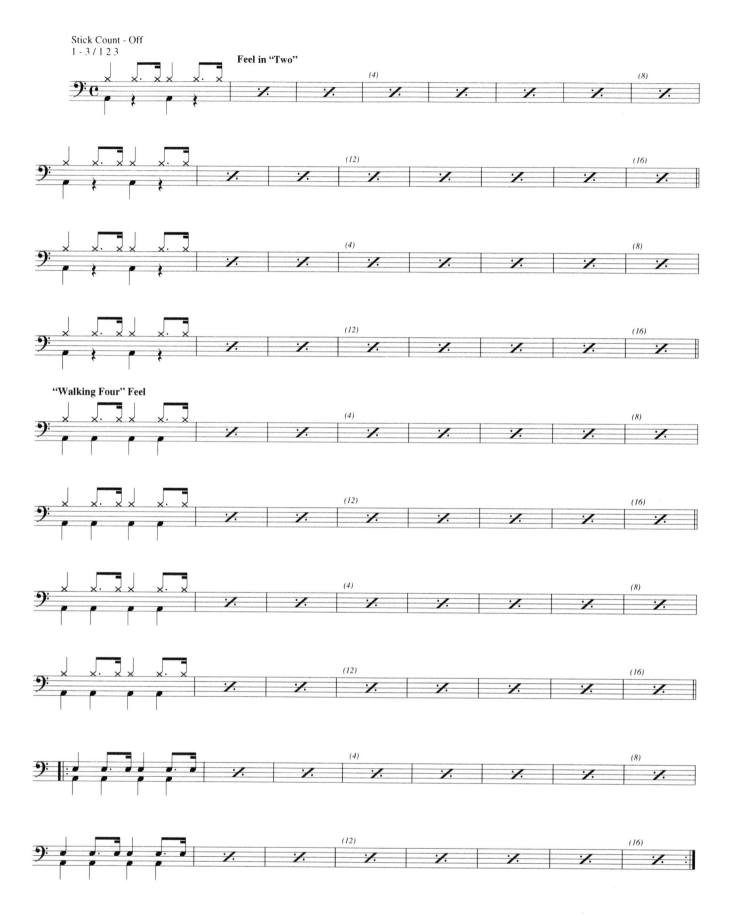

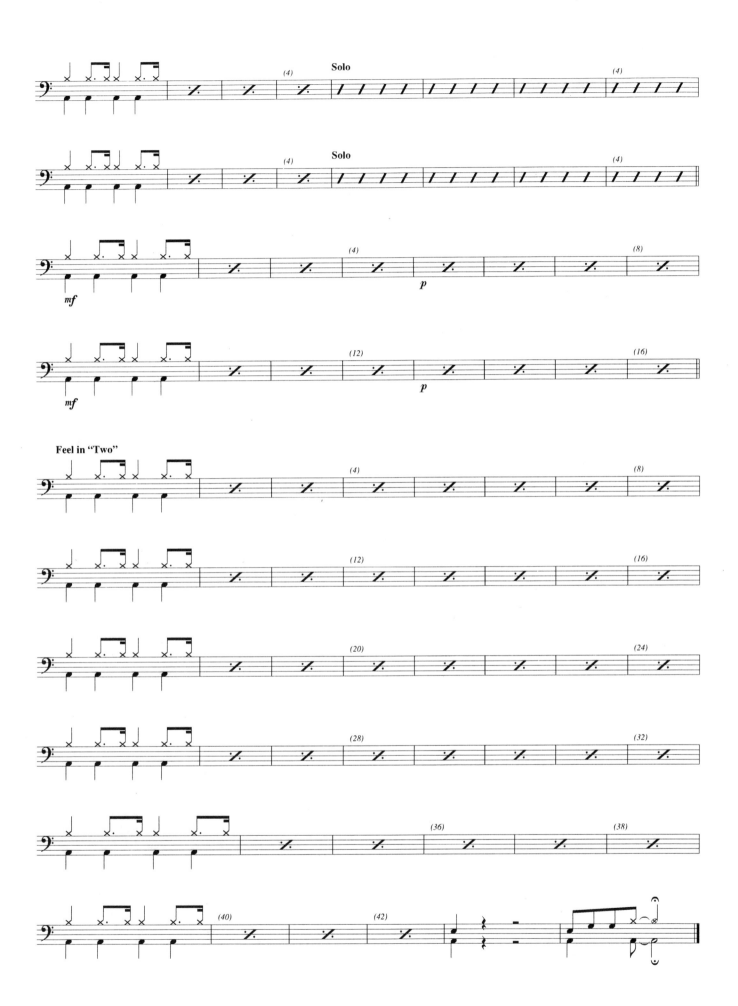

Terry's Tune

Music by TERRY PEARCE

MMO CD 5006
Cassette 4075

Comin' Home Baby

Words and Music by BEN TUCKER & BOB DOROUGH

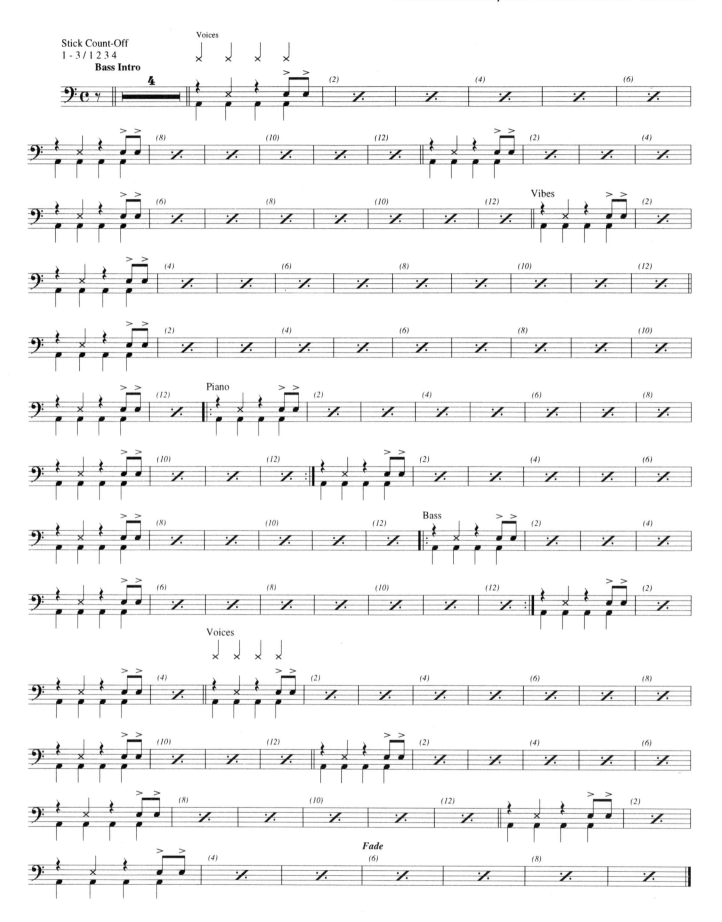

The Girl From Ipanema

Music by ANTONIO CARLOS JOBIM
English Lyrics by NORMAN GIMBEL
Original Lyrics by VINICIUS De MORAES

Drum Pad Stick Skin

You're the soloist with these trio, quartet and quintet groups as they play rock, soul, ballad, jazz, latin and pop renditions of these great songs.

Listen to the recorded drummer. Then add your solo to complete the recording on the version minus drums.

Includes the complete drum charts for all the songs.

5006

The Kenny Smith Trio
The Mike Abene Quartet
The Mauricio Smith Quintet
Dee Dee Bridgewater, vocals

MMO CD 5006
Cassette 4075

16

The Beat Goes On
Song for My Father
Watermelon Man
John Brown's Body
Terry's Tune
The Girl from Ipanema
Comin Home Baby